THE FRIENDS

to C.G.

HarperCollins*Publishers*
77–85 Fulham Palace Road,
Hammersmith, London W6 8JB

www.harpercollins.co.uk

First published by HarperCollins*Publishers* 2008
1

A catalogue record of this book
is available from the British Library

ISBN-13 978 0 00 727843 5
ISBN-10 0 00 727843 8

Printed and bound in China by Leo Paper Products Limited

THE FRIENDS

The GARLIC is a friend of the CARROTS the CARROTS are friends of the POTATO the ONION is fickle and cannot decide where her loyalties lie and has hence formed a **LOVELESS** but **PRACTICAL** alliance with everyone except the BROCCOLI. Do not ask about the BROCCOLI it will only **MAKE YOU CRY**

FRIENDSHIP

The LOBSTER of LOVELINESS

May the Lobster of Loveliness
always swim beside you through
the ever flowing waters of
your **LIFE**

... but not <u>so</u> DIFFERENT that you become a Menace to Society and they have to take you off to the HEAD HOSPITAL and conduct experiments on your BRAIN.

That would just be <u>too</u> DIFFERENT, O.K?

DARE to be DIFFERENT

The GENTLE IAINS

We are GENTLE, we are KIND
and we are LOVELY *

*but sometimes we want to tell
everyone to just BUGGER OFF

Things You Can Do With It

1, Sew it onto your swimming costume like an amazing swimming award (but don't get it wet because it isn't waterproof.)

2, "Accidentally" drop it on the ground in front of people you want to impress.

3, See if you can use it as a bus pass. It does say you're very kind, after all.

4, Keep it in your pocket and, if anyone says you're not very kind, get it out and show it to them then say "SO THERE!"

The BADGE of KINDNESS

VERY KIND

This is a special Badge of Kindness
for you to cut out and keep

THE FRIENDS

THE FRIENDS can connect in a mysterious way without even speaking.

Perhaps they have AMAZING MAGICAL POWERS.

Perhaps they are both just PECULIAR IN THE HEAD.

And in the New Administration, they ordered all the people through the 'SENSIBLE' MACHINE.

But some were so INSANE that they ESCAPED the Treatment, for nothing could be done to take their LUNACY away.

CONGRATULATIONS to a fellow escapee!

The `SENSIBLE' MACHINE

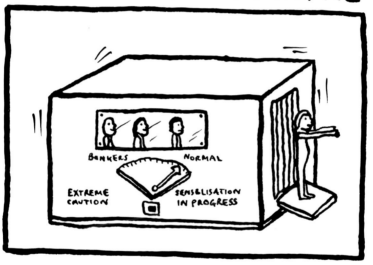

The RABBIT of TRUTH

You are WONDERFUL. Even the all-knowing Rabbit of Truth agrees. If you don't believe me - just ask him.

Marvellous marvellous
lovely lovely lovely
wonderful wonderful
wonderful YOU!

(dressed as a banana)

WONDERFUL YOU

BEST FRIENDS

So close are they that they will do **ANYTHING** for one another.

Well, anything except for <u>**THAT**</u>

"Your life will be **LONG** and **HAPPY**. Great **WEALTH** will be yours and **LOVE** will follow you **ALWAYS**.

Oh, hang on, it's **YOU** ... Sorry... You will wander **NAKED** through the woods with cider... **CIDER**... as your only friend."

The FORTUNE TELLER

The GIRL with the LOVELY HEART

This is the Piece of Loveliness of which I Speak

And when they shone their MIGHTY TORCHES and looked inside her HEART, the People were ASTONISHED.

For, lo, they saw before them a tiny GLOWING piece of GOLDEN LOVELINESS — the rarest and most PRECIOUS of all the planet's Treasures.

Beware the Deadly Donkey
Falling slowly from the sky
You can CHOOSE the way
You LIVE, my friend
But not the way you DIE

The DEADLY DONKEY

FRIENDS

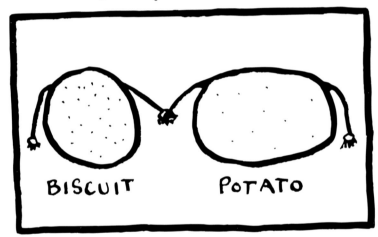

The BISCUIT will only dare
to be just a BISCUIT when
it is with its TRUE FRIEND
the POTATO

THE END